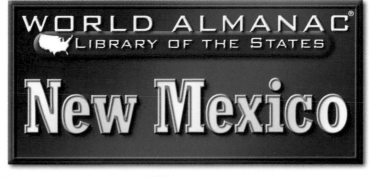

WORLD ALMANAC® LIBRARY OF THE STATES

New Mexico

LAND OF ENCHANTMENT

by Michael Burgan

WORLD ALMANAC® LIBRARY

Please visit our web site at: **www.worldalmanaclibrary.com**
For a free color catalog describing World Almanac® Library's list of high-quality books and multimedia programs, call 1-800-848-2928 (USA) or 1-800-387-3178 (Canada). World Almanac® Library's fax: (414) 332-3567.

Library of Congress Cataloging-in-Publication Data

Burgan, Michael.
    New Mexico, land of enchantment / by Michael Burgan.
        p. cm. — (World Almanac Library of the states)
    Includes bibliographical references and index.
    Summary: Text and illustrations present the history, geography, people, politics and government, economy, customs, and attractions of New Mexico.
    ISBN 0-8368-5156-0 (lib. bdg.)
    ISBN 0-8368-5327-X (softcover)
    1. New Mexico—Juvenile literature. [1. New Mexico.] I. Title. II. Series.
F796.3.B87   2003
978.9—dc21   2002191008

First published in 2003 by
World Almanac® Library
330 West Olive Street, Suite 100
Milwaukee, WI 53212 USA

Copyright © 2003 by World Almanac® Library.

A Creative Media Applications Production
Design: Alan Barnett, Inc.
Copy editor: Laurie Lieb
Fact checker: Joan Verniero
Photo researcher: Linette Ellis Mathewson
World Almanac® Library project editor: Tim Paulson
World Almanac® Library editors: Mary Dykstra, Gustav Gedatus, Jacqueline Laks Gorman, Lyman Lyons
World Almanac® Library art direction: Tammy Gruenewald
World Almanac® Library graphic designers: Scott M. Krall, Melissa Valuch

Photo credits: pp. 4-5 © Royalty-Free/CORBIS; p. 6 (bottom left) © ArtToday, (top right) © ArtToday, (bottom right) © Bruce Coleman; p. 7 (top) © ArtToday, (bottom) © AP/Wide World Photos; p. 9 © Bruce Coleman; p. 10 © North Wind Picture Archives; p. 11 © Hulton Archive/Getty Images; p. 12 © N. Carter/North Wind Picture Archives; p. 13 © Craig Lovell Eagle Visions Photographs; p. 14 © Photri, Inc.; p. 15 © AP/Wide World Photos; p. 17 © John Elk III; p. 18 © John Elk III; p. 19 © Bruce Coleman; p. 20 (left to right) © ArtToday, © Maresa Pryor/Danita Delimont, Agent, © ArtToday; p. 21 (left to right) © John Elk III, © Buddy Mays, © John Elk III; p. 23 © Tom Till; p. 26 © Bruce Coleman; p. 27 © Buddy Mays; p. 29 © John Elk III; p. 31 (top) © Wally McNamee/CORBIS, (bottom) © John Elk III; p. 32 © Photri, Inc.; p. 33 © Craig Lovell Eagle Visions Photographs; p. 34 © Bruce Coleman; p. 35 © John Elk III; p. 36 © Photri, Inc.; p. 37 (top) © Hulton Archive/Getty Images, (bottom) © Maresa Pryor/Danita Delimont, Agent; p. 38 © Hulton Archive/Getty Images; p. 39 © Photri, Inc.; p. 40 (top) © Hulton Archive/Getty Images, (bottom) © Buddy Mays/Travel Stock; p. 41 (top) © AP/Wide World Photos, (bottom) NASA; pp. 42-43 © North Wind Picture Archives; p. 44 (top) © ArtToday, (bottom) © Buddy Mays; p. 45 (top) © Buddy Mays, (bottom) © Bruce Coleman

Printed in the United States of America

1 2 3 4 5 6 7 8 9 07 06 05 04 03

New Mexico

Introduction	4
Almanac	6
History	8
The People	16
The Land	20
Economy & Commerce	24
Politics & Government	28
Culture & Lifestyle	32
Notable People	38
Time Line	42
State Events & Attractions	44
More About New Mexico	46
Index	47

Land of Contrasts

New Mexico is famous for its high deserts and mountain ranges, but the state is more than just sand and rocky peaks. The Rio Grande flows through New Mexico, providing water for crops and recreation. And in this desert land, some high elevations receive 300 inches (762 centimeters) of snow each year. The striking natural beauty of New Mexico helps explain its nickname, "Land of Enchantment."

Along with this scenery, New Mexico boasts a rich history. The state is home to three distinct cultures. The Anasazi, a major Native American people of the old Southwest, built communities high in the mountains. Today, Indian nations that trace their roots to the Anasazi and other Native peoples still live in New Mexico. The state also has a large Hispanic population; some of these people are the descendants of Spanish settlers who came to New Mexico hundreds of years ago. The last major group to reach the state was the Anglos — English-speaking Americans. Today, these three cultural groups shape New Mexico's political and social life.

New Mexico became a U.S. territory in 1850 after the Mexican-American War (1846–1848), but it did not become a state until 1912. For many years, this remote part of the country did not draw many new citizens. During World War II, however, the U.S. government began testing weapons in New Mexico's deserts. People flocked to the state to work for government agencies and defense companies, and that growth continues today.

New Mexico is not just a center for research and high technology. The state offers wonderful sunlight and the isolation many artists crave for their work. Santa Fe and Taos are important U.S. arts centers.

Contrasts between artists and scientists, snowy peaks and desert sands, and the state's distinct cultural traditions are just part of New Mexico's enchanting ways.

▶ Map of New Mexico showing the interstate highway system, as well as major cities and waterways.

▼ Desert plants struggle to survive in the shifting dunes of New Mexico's White Sands National Monument.

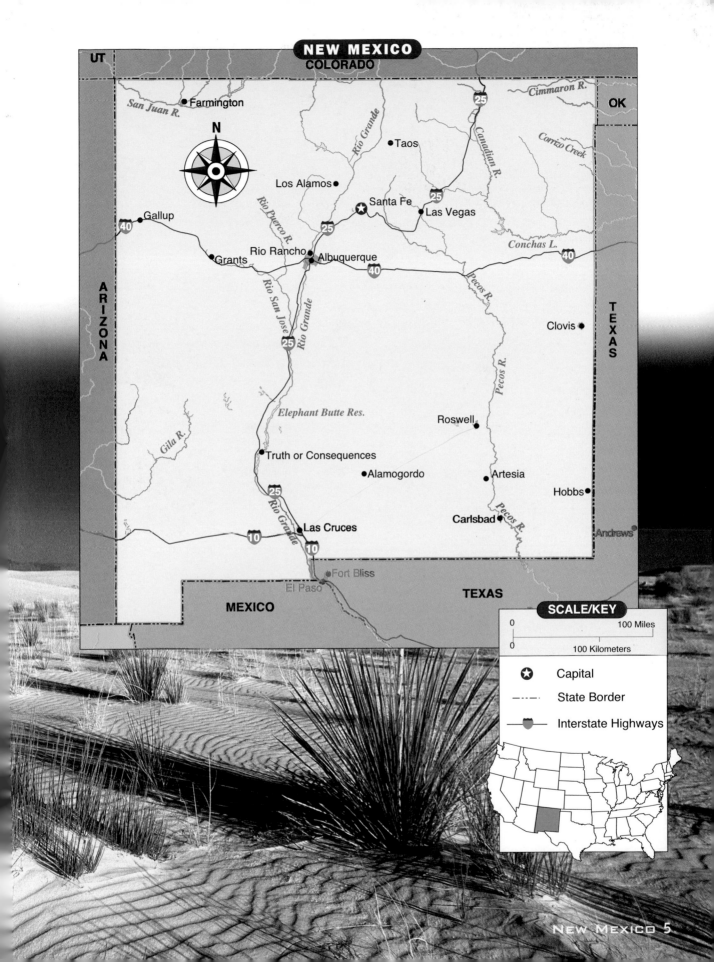

NEW MEXICO

COLORADO

UT

OK

San Juan R.
Farmington

N

Taos

Los Alamos

Rio Grande

Cimmaron R.

Corrizo Creek

Canadian R.

25

25

Santa Fe

Las Vegas

25

Conchas L.

Gallup

40

Rio Puerco R.

25

40

Rio Rancho

Albuquerque

Grants

Rio San Jose

40

Rio Grande

Clovis

A
R
I
Z
O
N
A

Pecos R.

T
E
X
A
S

Gila R.

Elephant Butte Res.

Roswell

Pecos R.

Truth or Consequences

Alamogordo

Artesia

Hobbs

25

Carlsbad

Pecos R.

Andrews

10

Rio Grande

Las Cruces

10

Fort Bliss

El Paso

TEXAS

MEXICO

SCALE/KEY

0   100 Miles

0   100 Kilometers

⭐ Capital

-··-··- State Border

━━ Interstate Highways

Fast Facts

New Mexico (NM), Land of Enchantment

Entered Union
January 6, 1912 (47th state)

Capital	Population
Santa Fe	62,203

Total Population (2000)
1,819,046 (36th most populous state) — *Between 1990 and 2000, the state's population increased 20.1 percent.*

Largest Cities	Population
Albuquerque	448,607
Las Cruces	74,267
Santa Fe	62,203
Rio Rancho	51,765
Roswell	45,293

Land Area
121,356 square miles (314,312 square kilometers) (5th largest state)

State Motto
Crescit Eundo — *Latin for "It Grows As It Goes"*

State Songs
"O, Fair New Mexico" *by Elizabeth Garrett, adopted in 1917;* "Asi Es Nuevo Méjico" *by Amadeo Lucero, adopted in 1971.*

State Ballad
"The Land of Enchantment" *by Michael Martin Murphy, Chick Raines, and Don Cook, adopted in 1989.*

State Bird
Roadrunner — *This relative of the cuckoo can run at speeds up to 15 miles (24 km) per hour.*

State Fish
New Mexico cutthroat trout

State Insect
Tarantula hawk wasp — *A mother tarantula hawk wasp kills a spider with her stinger, then uses the dead spider as a "nest" for a single egg.*

State Mammal
Black bear

State Flower
Yucca

State Tree
Piñon

State Grass
Blue grama

State Vegetables
Chile (pepper) and frijoles (beans)

State Gem
Turquoise

State Fossil
Coelophysis — *This fast-footed, meat-eating dinosaur roamed New Mexico more than 200 million years ago.*

PLACES TO VISIT

Acoma Pueblo, *Acoma*
Named for the people who built it, Acoma Pueblo sits on a flat, stony hill called a mesa about 350 feet (107 meters) high. The village is also known as "Sky City." The Acoma have lived here since at least the eleventh century. The pueblo also features a church built by the Spanish in 1639.

Carlsbad Caverns National Park, *Carlsbad*
One of the largest cave systems in the world, Carlsbad Caverns has about eighty caves. The public can explore several of the caves and their underground "rooms."

El Rancho de las Golondrinas, *Santa Fe*
This eighteenth-century ranch was once the last stop on the El Camino Real, a roadway that linked Santa Fe with Mexico City, Mexico. Today, the ranch is a "living museum," offering a look at what life was like for Spanish settlers more than 250 years ago.

For other places and events, see p. 44. For other places and events, see p. 44.

BIGGEST, BEST, AND MOST

- With an elevation of about 7,000 feet (2,134 m), Santa Fe is the highest capital city in the United States. Santa Fe is also the oldest capital city in the United States.

- White Sands National Monument is the world's largest gypsum field. It is made of some 275 square miles (712 sq km) of gypsum.

STATE FIRSTS

- 1598 El Camino Real, the "real highway," was the first major road in colonial America. The road linked Santa Fe with Mexico City.

- 1610 The Palace of the Governors in Santa Fe is the oldest public building in continuous use in the United States.

- 1945 The world's first atomic bomb was tested at the Trinity Site, in the desert outside Alamogordo, on July 16.

What Happened at Roswell?

A rancher finds broken objects scattered on the ground. The U.S. military first says the debris came from the crash of an unidentified flying object (UFO). Just four hours later, the military says the parts are from a weather balloon. Sounds like the start of a science fiction movie, but these events actually happened in 1947 in Roswell. Today, some people still believe that at least one alien spaceship crashed in Roswell and that the government refuses to admit it. Each year, Roswell attracts thousands of tourists convinced that humans are not alone in the universe.

A Cub Survives

The bear cub that became the model for Smokey Bear, the symbol of fire safety in the United States, was found trapped in a tree in Lincoln National Forest, in southeastern New Mexico. A forest fire in 1950 had destroyed the cub's home. Originally called Hot Foot Teddy, the cub received medical treatment in Santa Fe before moving to his new home at the National Zoo in Washington, D.C.

WHY?
remember—
only you can **PREVENT FOREST FIRES!**

Building A Diverse State

> We come as friends, to better your condition and make you part of the Republic of the United States.
>
> — *General Stephen Kearny to the people of New Mexico, 1846*

More than ten thousand years ago, Native Americans arrived in what is now New Mexico. Some of these people are called the Sandia, named for the Sandia Mountains, where scientists have found their remains. Over the centuries that followed, new tribes settled in the region, creating some of the most important Native cultures found in the United States.

One notable Native group was the Mogollon, who lived in southwestern New Mexico and Arizona starting about twenty-five hundred years ago. Unlike the Sandia, the Mogollon were not nomads — wandering hunters — but farmers who raised corn, beans, and squash. A later group of Mogollon, the Mimbres, are famous for their pottery. After the Mogollon, a new people settled in the Southwest — the Anasazi. They created the huge pueblos that still dot central New Mexico. These Native Americans were the ancestors of the Hopi, Zuni, and Pueblo peoples who live in the region today.

The Anasazi were skilled basket weavers, potters, and farmers. They built their homes out of adobe, a mixture of mud and straw, or stones. Inside, up to one thousand people could live in a complex with hundreds of rooms. The Anasazi held their religious ceremonies in special underground chambers called kivas. The Anasazi reached their peak in New Mexico about A.D. 1100. But within two hundred years, they began to leave their villages and scatter across the Southwest. They built new pueblos and began to farm again. Only a few of these later communities, such as the one in Taos, are still home to the descendants of the Anasazi.

After the decline of the Anasazi, the Navajo (Dineh) and

Native Americans of New Mexico
Anasazi
Apache
Hopi
Mogollon (including Mimbres)
Navajo (Dineh)
Pueblo (including Acoma, Keres, Tewa, Tiwa, and Zia)
Sandia
Ute Mountain
Zuni

DID YOU KNOW?

The Anasazi pueblos had flat roofs. The apartments were arranged on top of each other, forming the shape of large steps, and people used ladders to climb from one floor to the next.

Apache came to New Mexico. Both groups were nomads, although they gradually adopted some of the Anasazi's culture and became farmers. Later, many Navajo turned to herding sheep for their livelihood.

The Spanish Arrive

In 1539, a Spanish priest named Marcos de Niza and a slave named Estevanico led a small party northward from Mexico. Father Niza was one of the first Europeans to enter New Mexico. The Spanish had come to the "New World" for riches — gold, silver, and jewels — and to convert the Native people to Christianity. Father Niza hoped to continue that quest in what is now the U.S. Southwest.

In New Mexico, Niza thought he had discovered Cibola, a land said to have seven cities filled with fabulous wealth. Instead, he had found Hawikúh, home to members of the Zuni nation. This first encounter did not go well: The Zuni killed Estevanico, who had entered the city as a scout.

DID YOU KNOW?

Today, part of the Navajo reservation lies in the northwest corner of New Mexico, while many Apache live on two reservations in the state. Another tribe, the Ute Mountain, has part of its reservation in northwest New Mexico. The nineteen Pueblo tribes also have their own reservation.

▼ The Anasazi villages at Chaco Culture National Historic Park were built about one thousand years ago.

Still, the priest returned to Mexico with tales of great riches. In a report to Spanish leaders, the priest wrote, "It appears to be a very beautiful city; the houses are . . . all of stone, with their stories and terraces." The next year, the soldier and explorer Francisco Vásquez de Coronado ventured to Hawikúh. He and his troops found only adobe homes, not gold and jewels. Coronado left New Mexico in disgust, still hoping to find Cibola.

During the next fifty years, several groups of Spaniards traveled to New Mexico, but the first settlement did not begin until 1598. Don Juan de Oñate led a group of Spaniards who lived for a short time with the Tewa at San Juan Pueblo. The settlers then began building their own town, San Gabriel. Within a few months, however, war broke out between the Spaniards and the Acoma. Oñate ordered an attack on their Sky City. Hundreds of Native Americans were killed, and hundreds more were captured and forced into slavery. The settlers' actions helped prevent any Native American attacks for years to come.

▼ **This plaza marked the end of the Santa Fe Trail.**

Spanish and Mexican Rule

More Spaniards came to New Mexico. Most were priests, who set up missions where they could convert the Native Americans to Christianity. By 1608, the priests claimed to have won eight thousand converts. The Spanish called the native people of New Mexico Pueblo Indians. *Pueblo* is the Spanish word for "village."

In 1610, the Spanish moved their capital from San Gabriel to Santa Fe, and the king's officials took direct control of New Mexico. The missionary work continued for most of the seventeenth century, but by 1680, the Pueblo Indians had tired of the priests and their new religion. The Pueblo rebelled and drove the Spanish out of New Mexico.

A shaman, or Native religious leader, named Popé organized this successful rebellion of 1680. Popé refused to convert to Christianity or stop performing traditional religious acts, and he was arrested and beaten for this defiance. Popé planned the rebellion by sending messengers to other pueblos. On August 10, the Native Americans launched raids against the Spanish, then marched on Santa Fe. After the Pueblo victory, Popé tried to erase all traces of the Spanish, and he began to rule as a dictator. The alliance between the different Native American groups soon began to crumble. In 1692, Spanish troops regained control of Santa Fe, and within two years, the rebellion was over.

During the years of Spanish rule in New Mexico, new settlers came from both Mexico and Spain to farm and ranch. Albuquerque, named for a Spanish leader, was founded in 1706 and became one of the major towns in New Mexico. By 1800, about thirty thousand Europeans lived in the colony. New Mexico was controlled by a governor, appointed by the Spanish king or his representative in Mexico. Farther south, in Mexico, the colonists began demanding more rights from Spain. Finally, in 1821, the Mexicans won a revolution that gave them their freedom. New Mexico became part of the newly independent country of Mexico.

William Becknell

Called the "Father of the Santa Fe Trail," William Becknell was a frontiersman, politician, and trader. Born around 1788 in Virginia, Becknell fought against Native Americans during the War of 1812, then settled in Missouri. In 1821, he recruited a small trading party to go to New Mexico. These men were the first Americans allowed to trade in the territory, since the Spanish had not allowed foreign traders in New Mexico. After making money on the trip, Becknell returned home, then took a wagon train across the Great Plains to Santa Fe, marking the start of the Santa Fe Trail. Starting in 1822, the trail was the major trade link between New Mexico and the central United States until railroads arrived during the 1870s. Becknell eventually moved to Texas, where he died in 1856.

The Americans Take Over

A few years before the Mexican Revolution, the first Americans reached New Mexico. These Anglos — non-Spanish, English-speaking people — were mostly trappers. By the 1820s, more Americans reached the region along the Santa Fe Trail, a path from Missouri to Mexico. Ranchers drove cattle along the road, and traders brought goods to sell. Some Anglos saw they could make money in New Mexico and stayed in the region. Many of these Americans considered themselves superior to the native New Mexicans, both Spanish and Indian.

After the Mexican Revolution, New Mexicans ran their affairs mostly as they chose. That freedom, however, did not last long. In the United States, many politicians and business owners wanted to take control of California, which was part of Mexico. In 1846, the United States started a war with Mexico, and General Stephen Kearny marched U.S. troops into Santa Fe. Kearny drafted a new set of laws for the territory and began the process of making New Mexico a part of the United States. He named Charles Bent, of Taos, governor of the region. Bent, however, did not serve long as governor. A group of New Mexicans and Pueblo Indians who opposed U.S. rule attacked and killed him in January 1847.

▼ The ancient cliff dwellers at what is now called Bandelier National Monument pulled up the ladders that led to their homes when facing enemy attack.

Troops from Santa Fe helped restore order in Taos and end the rebellion.

The Mexican War ended in 1848, with the United States acquiring what is now New Mexico, California, Texas, Arizona, Nevada, Colorado, and Utah. A few years later, the U.S. government bought a small strip of land from Mexico that added to New Mexico's southern border. The present borders of the state were set by 1863. Until then, the New Mexico territory included present-day New Mexico, Arizona, parts of southern Colorado, southern Utah, and a portion of southwest Nevada. New Mexico attracted people looking to farm or sell goods, along with Americans looking for adventure in the West.

▲ Rock drawings like these, called petroglyphs, can be found across northern New Mexico. They were painted by the Anasazi hundreds of years ago.

War and the Wild West

During the Civil War (1861–1865), some New Mexicans backed the Confederacy. Most lived in the southern part of the territory. Other New Mexicans remained loyal to the Union. The first major Civil War battle in the Southwest territories took place at Valverde in February 1862. A force of Texans clashed with Union soldiers and volunteers from New Mexico and Colorado. A month later, Confederate troops took over Albuquerque and Santa Fe, but Union forces drove them out of New Mexico.

After the war ended in 1865, more Anglos came to New Mexico. Texas cattle ranchers moved to the territory, competing with sheep ranchers for land. Miners also came, looking for gold and other important minerals. The miners and cowboys who worked on the ranches helped make New Mexico part of the "Wild West." Most men carried guns, and arguments could turn deadly. Cimarron was especially known for attracting outlaws, and going three days without a killing was big news in the local papers.

Violence came as U.S. troops had begun forcing New Mexico's Plains Indians onto reservations during the 1860s. The process lasted until the 1880s. The Pueblo were largely ignored by U.S. officials. The government did not prevent Anglos from taking their land, and the Pueblos received little or no government aid. New Mexico's Native Americans were denied the right to vote until 1948.

Many miners did not stay long in New Mexico. After taking all the gold and silver they could find, they moved

Buffalo Bill's Wild West Show

During the 1880s, Buffalo Bill Cody organized a famous "Wild West" exhibit that toured the United States and Europe, giving city residents a taste of Western life. He recruited many of the members of his show in Cimarron, including the expert shooter Annie Oakley.

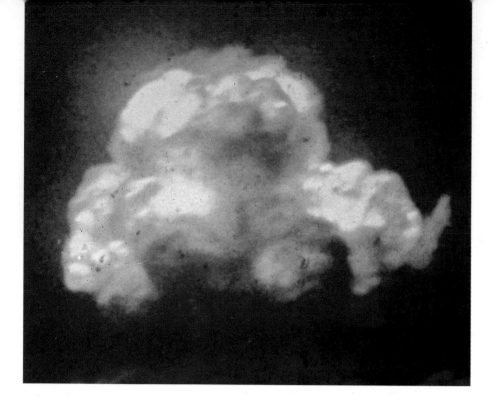

In 1945, scientists watched from more than five miles away as the world's first atomic bomb was tested at the Trinity Site, near Alamogordo. The bright light created by the explosion could be seen for more than 150 miles.

on, creating ghost towns. Ranching, however, remained an important source of income. Conflicts between competing cattle ranchers and merchants sometimes led to violence, such as the Lincoln County War (1878–1881). Slowly, the government restored order to New Mexico.

Statehood and Beyond

In 1912, New Mexico was admitted to the Union as the forty-seventh state. Before then, some Americans questioned the loyalty of non-Anglo New Mexicans. But during the Spanish-American War of 1898, Hispanics had proved their people's devotion to the United States by serving with Teddy Roosevelt's famous "Rough Riders." Later, during World War I (1914–1918), Hispanics and Native Americans made up one-third of the troops that New Mexico contributed to the war effort.

Hispanics remained a large part of the population and played an important role in business and government. The state's second governor was Hispanic. In small villages, however, poor Hispanics struggled to survive. The Great Depression of the 1930s threatened to end their way of life, but programs started under President Franklin Roosevelt's New Deal helped the villagers. Dams built during the Depression were particularly important, providing water for new farmlands.

DID YOU KNOW?

In 1940, Albuquerque had a population of a little more than 35,000. By 1955, it had grown to 175,000, thanks mostly to new defense-related industries.

World War II (1939–1945) gave some villagers the chance to move to cities and find work. The war also brought a large number of educated Anglos to the state, to work on defense programs. The most important was the development of the atomic bomb, which was built at Los Alamos. After the war, scientists came to develop missiles at the White Sands Missile Range and to work at government laboratories.

Appeal of an Enchanted Land

Government jobs provided work for native New Mexicans and others who flocked to the state. But not everyone came to work for the government. After World War II, New Mexico attracted a growing number of artists and writers. Some had come even earlier, but the migration began to climb during the 1950s and 1960s. The state's isolation and scenery also appealed to people who were looking for an alternative lifestyle. Some of these settlers opposed the Vietnam War (1964–1973) and wanted to separate themselves from American society. Many of these newcomers lived in the north, near Santa Fe and Taos.

New Mexico remains an art center. It also continues to attract people looking to get away from the fast-paced life of the East and West Coasts. This growth, combined with the desert climate, has led to problems providing citizens with enough water. In 2001, the state government spent more than $7 million on water projects to help keep the water flowing in this enchanted — and popular — land.

Rocket Man

Called the founder of modern rocketry, Robert Goddard helped make New Mexico a center for research and technology. Born in 1882 in Worcester, Massachusetts, Goddard experimented with rockets that burned liquid fuel. In 1930, he moved to Roswell, where the desert offered a good climate and plenty of space to continue his work. His backers included Charles Lindbergh, the first pilot to fly solo across the Atlantic Ocean. Working in New Mexico, Goddard became the first person to launch a liquid-fueled rocket that traveled faster than the speed of sound. He also perfected techniques for sending his rockets to high altitudes and keeping them on a steady course. During World War II, Goddard closed his operations in Roswell to work for the U.S. government.

Left: Dr. Robert H. Goddard is shown at his laboratory in Roswell in 1938 with one of the rockets he developed. Goddard fired the world's first liquid-fueled rocket in 1926.

Three in One

> There was now great perplexity for a national emblem. . . .
> I recommended the eagle, but they at last agreed upon two
> clasped hands in sign of brotherhood and amity with all nations.
>
> — *American trader Thomas James, in* Three Years Among the
> Indians and Mexicans, *recalling when New Mexicans learned
> about Mexico's independence from Spain, 1821*

Although New Mexico's population is small, it has grown quickly in recent decades. From 1990 to 2000, the state added more than 300,000 people, a growth rate of 20.1 percent. Most New Mexicans — about 75 percent in 2000 — live in urban areas. The largest of these are in the north-central part of the state, near Albuquerque and Santa Fe. The northwest corner and the southwest corner also have large pockets of residents.

The people of New Mexico are often divided into three major groups: Native American, Hispanic, and Anglo. These groups can overlap. In colonial times, Spanish settlers sometimes married Pueblo Indians; their offspring were called *mestizos*, or mixed children. Since coming to New Mexico in the early nineteenth century, Anglos have married both Hispanics and Native Americans. New Mexico has seen

Age Distribution in New Mexico
(2000 Census)

Age	Population
0–4	130,628
5–19	434,231
20–24	121,291
25–44	516,100
45–64	404,571
65 & over	212,225

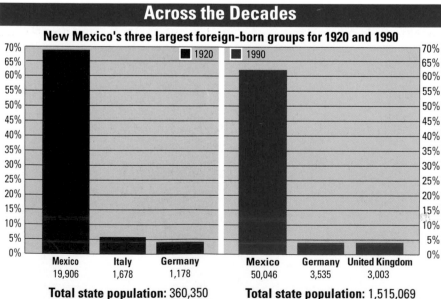

Across the Decades

New Mexico's three largest foreign-born groups for 1920 and 1990

	1920	1990
Mexico	19,906	50,046
Italy	1,678	
Germany	1,178	3,535
United Kingdom		3,003

Total state population: 360,350
Total foreign-born: 29,077 (8.1%)

Total state population: 1,515,069
Total foreign-born: 80,514 (5.3%)

Patterns of Immigration

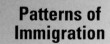

The total number of people who immigrated to New Mexico in 1998 was 2,199. Of that number, the largest immigrant groups were from Mexico (61.8%), India (5.3%), and China (3.5%).

a blending of the three peoples that is unique in the United States.

Within the three groups there are also distinct categories. The various Pueblo Indian groups are unrelated to the Apache and Navajo. Hispanics include descendants of original Spanish residents and more recent immigrants from Mexico. And the Anglo community features Americans from many different ethnic backgrounds.

▲ The corn dance is an important event at many pueblos.

The Native People

In 2000, Native Americans made up just under 10 percent of the population in New Mexico. Some live in the state's cities and towns, but a large number live on reservations and at the traditional pueblo communities. Most of the nineteen Pueblo Indian groups are centered in the northern half of the state, in a corridor that stretches roughly from Albuquerque to Taos. The Navajo Reservation, which extends from the northwest corner of New Mexico into Arizona and Utah, is the largest Indian reservation in the United States. The 2000 census showed that almost forty-five thousand Navajo live on the reservation in New Mexico. The state also has two Apache reservations — Jicarilla in the north and Mescalero in the south — as well as other reservations.

Heritage and Background, New Mexico   Year 2000

▶ Here is a look at the racial backgrounds of New Mexicans today. New Mexico ranks fortieth among all U.S. states with regard to African Americans as a percentage of the population.

Native Hawaiian and Other Pacific Islander
1,503
0.1%

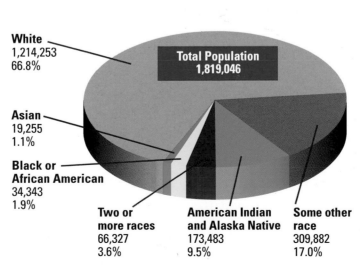

White
1,214,253
66.8%

Total Population
1,819,046

Asian
19,255
1.1%

Black or African American
34,343
1.9%

Two or more races
66,327
3.6%

American Indian and Alaska Native
173,483
9.5%

Some other race
309,882
17.0%

Note: 42.1% (765,386) of the population identify themselves as **Hispanic** or **Latino,** a cultural designation that crosses racial lines. Hispanics and Latinos are counted in this category as well as the racial category of their choice.

Hispanics

New Mexico has a larger percentage of Hispanics in its population than any other state. Most trace their roots to Spain and Mexico, though some come from Central and South America. In some counties, Hispanics are more than 50 percent of the population. Hispanic New Mexicans have played a large role in New Mexico's politics and economy. These New Mexicans have often had more power than any other group of Hispanics living in the United States. More recent immigrants from Mexico have had trouble reaching the same levels of influence.

Anglos

Today, Anglos live throughout New Mexico, mostly in the larger cities and towns. Although the last cultural group to

Educational Levels of New Mexico Workers (age 25 and over)	
Less than 9th grade	104,985
9th to 12th grade, no diploma	134,996
High school graduate, including equivalency	301,746
Some college, no degree or associate degree	326,925
Bachelor's degree	154,372
Graduate or professional degree	111,777

▼ Albuquerque is New Mexico's largest city and its business center.

reach the state, they are influential in all levels of society. After New Mexico became a state, the U.S. government tried to "Americanize" the Native Americans and Hispanics living in the region — make them more like English-speaking Americans with European roots.

The influence of the Anglos sometimes led to conflicts with the Native Americans and Hispanic New Mexicans. During the 1960s and 1970s, some New Mexicans formed political groups to challenge the power of the Anglos. Since then, the Anglo community has been more aware of the rights and cultures of all New Mexicans.

▲ Weaving by hand is an ancient New Mexican art still practiced today.

Religion

New Mexicans have a wide range of religious beliefs. At the pueblos and on the reservations, many Native Americans follow the spiritual practices their ancestors did hundreds of years ago. Some ceremonies are held in kivas, which tourists are not allowed to enter. The pueblos also celebrate feast days of different Roman Catholic saints. These celebrations feature dances and blend traditional religious practices with Catholicism.

The Spanish have traditionally been Catholic, and they brought this religion to New Mexico. Today, most Hispanic New Mexicans are Catholic. The Anglos brought a number of different Protestant faiths to the state. The two largest Protestant groups are the Baptists and the Methodists.

Education

Free public education began after the Anglos came to New Mexico. Earlier, education was provided by Catholic schools, and usually only the wealthy sent their children to school. Today, all children between the ages of five and eighteen are required to attend school, public or private.

New Mexico has a large number of people with advanced college degrees, thanks to the scientific jobs in the state. Leading colleges and universities include the University of New Mexico, which has its main campus in Albuquerque; New Mexico State University, in Las Cruces; and the College of Santa Fe.

An Unknown Presence

The Anglo community in New Mexico includes a small number of Jews. Some trace their roots to Jewish merchants who came to New Mexico during the nineteenth century, while others are more recent arrivals. Scholars are discovering that New Mexico has also had a small number of "hidden" Jewish residents for hundreds of years. They came with the Spanish settlers and had to pretend to be Catholic to avoid arrest, since the Spanish crown had outlawed their faith.

Mountain Peaks and Desert Sands

> The moment I saw the brilliant, proud morning sun
> shine high over the deserts of Santa Fe, something
> stood still in my soul and I started to attend.
>
> — *Author D. H. Lawrence,* Phoenix: The Posthumous Papers, *1936*

New Mexico is the fifth-largest state in the Union, with a land area of 121,356 square miles (314,312 sq km). The state has only 234 square miles (606 sq km) of inland water. Geographers often divide New Mexico into three major geographic regions: the Great Plains, the Rocky Mountains, and the High or Colorado Plateau. Some geographers include a fourth category, the range and basin, which combines the southern portions of the Rockies and the plateau region. Eighty-five percent of the state has an elevation of more than 4,000 feet (1,219 m).

The Great Plains

The Great Plains cover the eastern third of New Mexico. In the United States, this area of mostly flat, grassy land stretches from the Rocky Mountains eastward to Kansas, and as far north as North Dakota. The Great Plains region has a mixture of short and tall grasses, including the state grass, the blue grama. Some types of cacti also grow there. The Pecos River flows through the region into Texas, and the Canadian River cuts through its upper part.

Highest Point
Wheeler Peak
13,161 feet (4,011 m)
above sea level

▼ *From left to right:*
Rafters on the Rio Grande; a sandhill crane; the Taos Pueblo; cholla cactus; the poisonous Gila monster; inside a cave at Carlsbad Caverns.

In New Mexico, notable natural features in the Great Plains include Capulin Volcano National Monument and Carlsbad Caverns. Capulin was created by a volcano active about sixty thousand years ago. The caverns were once part of a huge inland sea that existed in New Mexico hundreds of millions of years ago.

The Rocky Mountains

The Rocky Mountains and related mountain chains cut through the center of New Mexico. The other mountain ranges include the Sangre de Cristo, the San Juan, and the Jemez. The Rio Grande also flows through the northern part of the region before entering the High Plateau. Valleys near the river provide land for agriculture. Wheeler Peak, the state's highest mountain, is located in the Sangre de Cristo chain near Taos.

This central region of New Mexico also features high mesas and steep cliffs where the Anasazi once lived. Bandelier National Monument, west of Santa Fe, has ruins of Anasazi homes. Another national monument in the area, Petroglyph, preserves ancient Native American rock carvings in land where lava once flowed, then hardened.

The High Plateau

The western third of New Mexico is the driest; the southwestern corner is the state's true desert region. Portions of the Chihuahuan and Sonoran Deserts cover this part of the state, with the Chihuahuan spilling over into the other two regions. But this part of New Mexico also has large areas of forest. Gila National Forest, which covers more than 3 million acres (1,214,100 hectares), is the largest national forest in the United States. The High Plateau also has two small rivers, the Gila in the south and the San Juan in the north.

DID YOU KNOW?

Elephant Butte Lake was formed in 1916 after a dam was placed across the Rio Grande.

Largest Lakes

Elephant Butte Lake
36,500 acres
 (14,772 hectares)

Navajo Lake
15,590 acres (6,309 ha)

Conchas Lake
9,600 acres (3,885 ha)

NEW MEXICO GEOGRAPHY

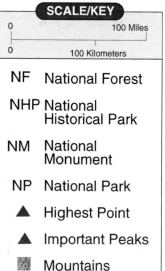
A notable physical feature of the northern part of the region is Shiprock, located near the Four Corners — the point where New Mexico, Colorado, Utah, and Arizona meet. This natural "statue," which stands more than 1,000 feet (305 m) high, was formed after a powerful volcanic eruption about twelve million years ago. Over time, water eroded the hardened lava to create this rock monument.

Plants and Animals

Although often considered a desert region, New Mexico has forests covering about one-quarter of its area. Trees include junipers, scrub oaks, aspens, and different types of pines — including the state tree, the piñon. Grasslands lie in southern New Mexico as well as in the Great Plains region.

The plants there include various wildflowers, yucca, and different kinds of cacti. Yucca and cacti are also found in the desert regions. Shrubs known as chaparral also grow in New Mexico's hills and mountains.

New Mexico is home to mountain lions, elk, rabbit, beavers, foxes, and various kinds of squirrels and wild mice. There are prairie dogs and lesser prairie-chickens on the Great Plains, and the mountains shelter black bears and bighorn sheep. Game birds, which are hunted for food, include wild turkeys and quail. Bald eagles and other birds come to New Mexico to spend the winter.

A number of different reptiles and amphibians live across New Mexico — horned lizards, a variety of frogs and toads, several kinds of rattlesnake, and the massasauga, another poisonous snake. In the spider family, black widows and tarantulas are both found in New Mexico. The state's rivers and streams are home to different kinds of trout and other fish often caught for food.

Major Rivers

Rio Grande
1,900 miles (3,057 km)

Pecos River
926 miles (1,490 km)

Canadian River
906 miles (1,458 km)

▼ To the Navajo, Shiprock is known as *Tsé Bit'A'í*—"rock with wings." The rock is a sacred Navajo site. It is illegal to climb it.

Ancient Ways, Modern Technology

> Holes and shafts and tunnels are dug into the earth or rock; silver and lead have come out of some, gold and copper out of others, disappointment out of the majority.
>
> — *Fredric M. Endlich, "The Heart of New Mexico,"* Harper's Weekly, *September 7, 1889*

One thousand years ago, the Anasazi farmed small plots of land near the Rio Grande. Hundreds of years later, their descendants and Spanish settlers raised crops on small fields in the mountains. Ranchers also raised sheep, and then cattle, on grassy ranges. Farming and ranching are still an important way of life — and source of money — for some New Mexicans. The Native Americans also mined turquoise, a blue gem they used in jewelry. Later, American miners came to take gold and silver from the ground. Today, miners still dig deep into the earth to pull out valuable minerals.

But New Mexican workers do more than follow old traditions. In gleaming high-tech factories, they produce electronic parts. Scientists develop weapons and other products for the U.S. government. More people work in the service industry than in any other part of the economy.

Wealth from the Land

Slightly more than fifteen thousand farms and ranches in New Mexico produce food for local residents and the world. Approximately nine thousand of these operations raise cows for meat and dairy products. In 2000, New Mexico ranked as the tenth leading producer of milk in the United States. Another thousand ranches and farms raise sheep and hogs. Livestock produces about three-quarters of New Mexico's total farm income.

The state's farmers grow a variety of grains, including wheat, corn, and sorghum, and hay to feed the livestock.

Top Employers
(of workers age sixteen and over)

Services	46.0%
Wholesale and retail trade	14.9%
Federal, state, and local government (including military)	8.0%
Construction	7.9%
Transportation, communication, and other public utilities	7.1%
Manufacturing	6.5%
Finance, insurance, and real estate	5.5%
Agriculture, forestry, fisheries, and mining	4.0%

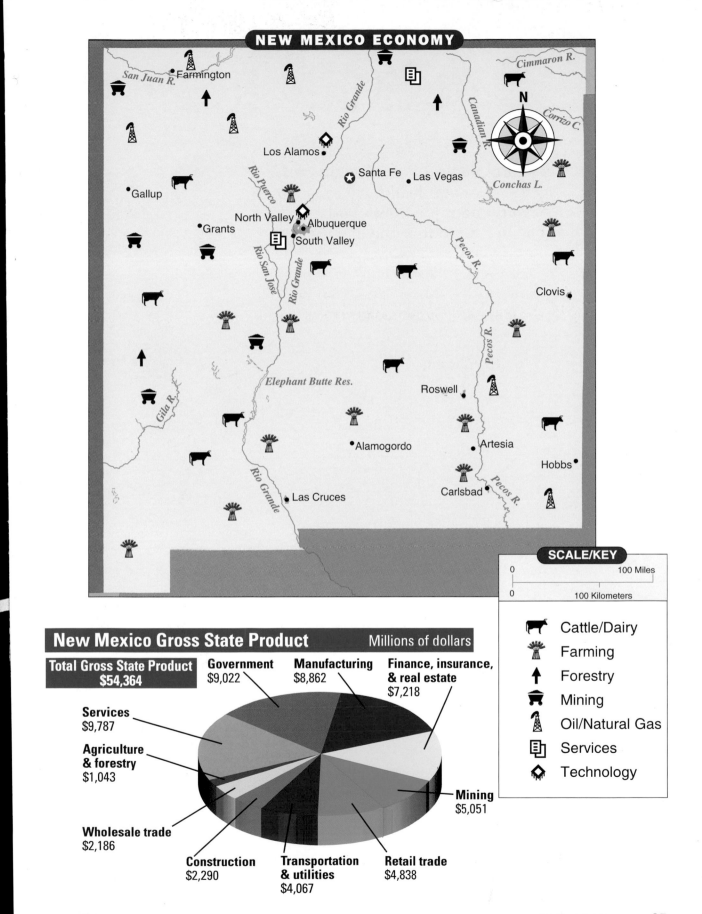

NEW MEXICO ECONOMY

Cimmaron R.
San Juan R. • Farmington
Rio Grande
Canadian R.
Corrizo C.
Los Alamos •
Santa Fe • Las Vegas
Conchas L.
• Gallup
Rio Puerco
North Valley
Grants • • Albuquerque
South Valley
Rio San Jose
Rio Grande
Pecos R.
Clovis •
Elephant Butte Res.
Pecos R.
Roswell
Gila R.
• Alamogordo
Artesia •
Hobbs •
Carlsbad •
Pecos R.
• Las Cruces

SCALE/KEY

0   100 Miles

0   100 Kilometers

Cattle/Dairy
Farming
Forestry
Mining
Oil/Natural Gas
Services
Technology

New Mexico Gross State Product   Millions of dollars

Total Gross State Product $54,364

Government $9,022

Manufacturing $8,862

Finance, insurance, & real estate $7,218

Services $9,787

Agriculture & forestry $1,043

Mining $5,051

Wholesale trade $2,186

Construction $2,290

Transportation & utilities $4,067

Retail trade $4,838

Farmers also raise trees, flowers, and shrubs in nurseries, to sell to homes and businesses. Other important crops are onions, pecans, peanuts, cotton, and New Mexico's most famous crop, the chile pepper. More than twenty-eight thousand tons (25,396 metric tons) were grown in 2000, and the state is the leading hot chile pepper producer in the nation. Processing crops and dairy goods produced in the state is one of New Mexico's leading industries.

In the state's forests and mountains, New Mexicans cut trees for lumber and mine the earth. In 2000, 100 million board feet (30.5 million board meters) of lumber were cut. Major natural resources include the fuels coal, natural gas, and petroleum. New Mexico ranks third nationally in natural gas production. The state leads the nation in the production of potash, a mineral used to make soap, fertilizer, and other products. Copper, silver, and gold are other important minerals in the state.

New Mexico's Native American reservations have valuable natural resources, such as uranium, that provide income for the Navajo. This mineral, however, is radioactive and can be deadly to humans. Many Navajo now oppose uranium mining on their land.

Manufacturing

In and around Albuquerque, several large firms produce high-technology goods, including semiconductors, which are used in computers and other electronic devices. In 2000, Intel, the world's largest semiconductor maker, began to expand its operation in Rio Rancho, planning to spend almost $2 billion. Intel and other electronics companies provide well-paying jobs for tens of thousands of New Mexicans. The Roswell area has several major manufacturing plants, including a bus factory and the world's largest mozzarella cheese company. As a leading producer of fuels and minerals, New Mexico is also a logical

▲ **The Spanish brought the first sheep to New Mexico, and the Pueblo and Navajo Indians used the sheep's wool in their weaving. Today, raising sheep is an important source of income for many New Mexicans.**

A Software Giant with Roots in New Mexico

One of the first personal computers ever sold, the Altair 8800, was built by a company based in Albuquerque. In 1975, the Altair began using a software program created by Bill Gates and Paul Allen, the founders of Microsoft. This software company was briefly based in New Mexico before moving to Bellevue, Washington.

place to refine and process these raw materials. The largest oil refinery in the state belongs to the Navajo Nation.

Research and development (R&D) are key to manufacturers. The companies need to research new ideas that can be developed into products or processes. New Mexico is a leader in R&D for high technology. The Sandia and Los Alamos National Laboratories play major roles in this field. Private companies add to these R&D efforts.

Transportation, Services, and Tourism

New Mexico is crisscrossed by three major interstate highways. Two of these meet in Albuquerque and are main north-south and east-west routes through the state. New Mexico has a total of 54,000 miles (86,886 km) of roads. The state has one major airport, in Albuquerque, and several smaller ones throughout the state.

The service industry can be broadly defined to include government services, retail, finances, health, education, and social welfare. The U.S. government is one of the largest employers in New Mexico, given the large number of military bases and research centers in the state. As the state's largest city, Albuquerque is the major center for the service industry, though Santa Fe has government-related services, and the state's other major cities also have service companies.

The tourism industry adds more than $3 billion each year to New Mexico's economy. Skiers flock to Taos and other Rocky Mountain resorts. Most tourists visit northern New Mexico, with its Native American and Wild West heritage, but Roswell is also a popular spot for people interested in UFOs and science fiction. The Native American people also receive guests who come to their casinos. Some of the casinos feature hotels and other activities besides gambling, and they employ more than five thousand people.

Made in New Mexico

Leading farm products and crops
Cattle and dairy products
Hay
Onions
Chiles
Greenhouse nursery
Pecans
Cotton
Corn

Other products
Foods
Machinery
Apparel
Lumber
Printing
Transportation
 Equipment
Electronics
Semiconductors

Major Airports		
Airport	**Location**	**Passengers per year (2000)**
Albuquerque International Sunport	Albuquerque	6,292,458

Preserving Rights and Order

> I knew [becoming part of the United States] would ultimately make our people freer and more independent than they ever could be under their former government.
>
> — *José Leandro Perea, rancher, 1846*

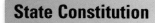

In 1846, General Stephen Kearny drafted the first laws for New Mexico under U.S. rule. Kearny blended some Mexican laws with U.S. laws, and he named the first American governor of the region. Four years later, New Mexico became a U.S. territory, a legal status just below a state. New Mexico officially joined the Union as a state in 1912.

Since then, New Mexico has had just one state constitution, which was adopted in 1911. This document outlines the operations of the state government and its basic laws. The constitution also contains a bill of rights, just as the U.S. Constitution does. New Mexicans can amend, or change, their constitution. Amendments require a majority vote in each house of the legislature; then a majority of voters must also approve them.

Like the U.S. government, the state government of New Mexico is divided into three branches: executive, legislative, and judicial. The executive branch carries out the laws, the legislative branch makes laws, and the judicial branch interprets the laws and how they are carried out.

The Executive Branch

The governor of New Mexico is the leader of the state's executive branch. The duties of the office include signing bills into law or vetoing bills passed by the legislature. The governor also prepares the budget for the state, pardons criminals, and is the commander of the state militia. New Mexico's governor can also appoint the members of many agencies, departments, and commissions in the executive branch, with the state senate's approval.

State Constitution

"**W**e, the people of New Mexico, grateful to Almighty God for the blessings of liberty, in order to secure the advantages of a state government, do ordain and establish this constitution."

— *Preamble to the New Mexico State Constitution*

Elected Posts in the Executive Branch		
Office	Length of Term	Term Limits
Governor	4 years	2 consecutive terms
Lieutenant Governor	4 years	2 consecutive terms
Secretary of State	4 years	2 consecutive terms
Attorney General	4 years	2 consecutive terms
State Treasurer	4 years	2 consecutive terms
State Auditor	4 years	none
Commissioner of Public Lands	4 years	2 consecutive terms
Public Regulation Commissioners	6 years	none

Other elected officials in the executive branch include the lieutenant governor, the secretary of state, the attorney general, the commissioner of public lands, and the state's auditor and treasurer. The lieutenant governor takes over when the governor is out of state or unable to perform the duties of the office. The lieutenant governor also breaks tie votes in the state senate. The secretary of state has many duties, including managing state elections. The attorney general enforces all the state's laws and represents New Mexico in legal matters. The commissioner of public lands is responsible for managing the money received from commercial activity on public lands, such as drilling for natural gas or mining. This money is then used to support schools and hospitals. The state auditor makes sure that taxes are properly collected and spent, while the treasurer acts as the state's banker, managing all the money the government receives. In 1996, New Mexican voters added a new office to the executive branch: public regulation commissioner. There are five such commissioners, who regulate insurance companies and utilities and make

▼ New Mexico is the only U.S. state with a round capitol building. The "Roundhouse," as it is known, opened in 1966.

sure all state corporations obey the laws. Voters also elect
ten members of the state board of education, while the
governor names five others.

The Legislative Branch

The New Mexico state legislature has two parts, the House
of Representatives and the Senate. The House has seventy
members, while the Senate has forty-two. The lawmakers
start their sessions each year in Santa Fe on the third
Tuesday of January. Sessions last up to sixty days in odd-
numbered years and thirty days in even-numbered years.
The state legislature can also meet in special sessions that
last no more than thirty days.

The legislature is responsible for drafting bills, which
become laws once they are signed by the governor. Certain
laws can be overturned by the voters if 10 percent of them
sign a petition calling for a special vote called a referendum.

The Judicial Branch

New Mexico's judicial branch has a variety of courts, with
judges elected by voters. The highest court is the Supreme
Court. This court reviews decisions made by lower courts
and decides if the decisions fairly apply the state's
constitution. Certain lower court decisions are
automatically appealed to the Supreme Court, such as
a conviction in a criminal trial that involves a possible
sentence of death. In other cases, the court decides which
cases it will hear on appeal. The Supreme Court has five
members, called justices. The head of the supreme court,
the chief justice, is chosen by the members of the court.

After the Supreme Court, New Mexico's next highest
court is the court of appeals. The ten judges on this court
meet in panels with three members in different cities in
the state. Beneath the court of appeals are thirteen district
courts, with a total of seventy-two judges. These courts hold
jury trials for all sorts of matters, both criminal and civil —
legal issues between individuals. Other courts are the

Legislature			
House	Number of Members	Length of Term	Term Limits
Senate	42 senators	4 years	None
House of Representatives	70 representatives	2 years	None

fifty-four magistrate courts, the Bernalillo County Metropolitan Court, the eighty-three municipal courts, and the thirty-three probate courts.

Local Government

Each state has local governments that handle such issues as education, maintaining roads and public spaces, collecting some taxes, and enforcing local and state laws. New Mexico has thirty-three counties. One town in each county serves as the seat, where the county government is located. In each county, voters elect county commissioners, the main government body for the county. Other elected county positions are clerk, treasurer, assessor, surveyor, sheriff, probate judge, and magistrate.

Within these thirty-three counties are 106 incorporated communities — cities and towns recognized by the state. Local, or municipal, government can be led by a mayor or a council or city commission, elected by voters. Some communities have both. Some also hire city or town managers to carry out decisions made by the local council or commission.

The Native Americans of New Mexico also have their own tribal governments. By U.S. law, Indian tribes operate as independent nations within the country's borders. Yet Native Americans are also U.S. citizens and can vote in local, state, and federal elections.

National Representation and Politics

Like all states, New Mexican voters elect two U.S. senators. The state also has three members in the U.S. House of Representatives, where representation is based on population. Notable politicians in New Mexico today include U.S. senators Pete Domenici and Jeff Bingaman and governor Bill Richardson. Domenici, a Republican, has held his seat since 1972. Bingaman, a Democrat, was first elected in 1982.

Joseph Montoya

One of New Mexico's best-known politicians, Joseph Montoya was born in 1915 in Peña Blanca. At 21, while still in law school, Montoya became the youngest person ever elected to the New Mexico House of Representatives in 1936. After holding several other state offices, Montoya was elected to the U.S. House of Representatives in 1957, and seven years later, he was elected a U.S. senator. In Congress, he supported protecting wilderness areas and promoted vocational education. Montoya left the Senate in 1977 and died the following year.

▶ Santa Fe's Palace of the Governors, once New Mexico's capitol building, is now a popular tourist attraction.

A Colorful Blend

> You never know in what obscure canyon or on what sun-baked mesa you will find an artist or scholar in exile.
>
> — *Author Conrad Richter,* The Mountain on the Desert, *1955*

Strolling by Santa Fe's Palace of the Governors, you can hear ranchers speaking English, politicians debating in Spanish, and Pueblo vendors recapping the day's sales in their native tongue. New Mexico has preserved its three heritages — Native American, Spanish, and Anglo — to create a vibrant culture found nowhere else in the United States.

Anglo culture, especially the English language, has dominated many aspects of life since New Mexico joined the Union. But at the pueblos and on the reservations, older Native Americans work to keep their languages and cultures alive. Hispanic and Latino Americans also preserve the best of their pasts, and the legal rights of Spanish speakers are protected by the state constitution. The sheer size of the Hispanic population also helps guarantee its role in shaping New Mexico's culture.

Art and Museums

New Mexico has impressive artistic wealth, given its small, scattered population. Since the nineteenth century, scholars have come to New Mexico to study the Native American ruins in the state. Their research has uncovered ancient art from the Anasazi and the Mimbres. Some of that art can be seen outdoors, at Petroglyph National Monument and at other sites in the northern part of the state. The Anasazi carved images of animals and symbols that were important to their religious

▼ A festive parade marks the Fiesta de Santa Fe.

beliefs. Even the position of an image on a rock — whether it faced east or west, north or south — had special meaning.

Examples of Native American art are also on display at museums around the state. Santa Fe is home to the Museum of Indian Arts and Culture, which features examples of Native American pottery, baskets, jewelry, and weaving. Albuquerque has the Indian Pueblo Cultural Center, which features all aspects of Pueblo culture as it exists today. On the pueblos and reservations, Native American artists use techniques passed on from one generation to another. The Navajo are famous for their silver jewelry and weaving, while visitors to Taos Pueblo can buy pottery created there. Some Native Americans also pursue painting, combining modern techniques with Indian themes. The best known of these painters is R. C. Gorman. He has been compared to some of the world's best modern painters, such as Pablo Picasso.

New Mexico's Hispano artists also look back to their past for some of their creations. *Santos*, religious images of saints carved or painted on wood, are found across northern New Mexico. Some carvers also create small animals. George López, of the small town of Cordova, won national recognition during the twentieth century for his carvings.

The Ancient Flute Player

One common petroglyph shows Kokopelli, an Anasazi figure with a hunched back playing a flute. Kokopelli was known as a trickster and someone who could bring good crops. He is also associated with music and dance. Today, modern images of Kokopelli are found all across New Mexico and other parts of the Southwest, from T-shirts to company signs.

López learned his skill from his father, and he then passed it on to his children. Other Hispano craftspeople have kept alive colonial ways of weaving. In small towns across New Mexico, tourists are often welcomed into the artists' homes to buy their work. The Spanish colonial tradition in New Mexican arts was formally recognized in 2002, with the opening of Santa Fe's Museum of Spanish Colonial Art.

Since the early twentieth century, New Mexico has been home to many famous Anglo artists. The best known is Georgia O'Keeffe, who painted the New Mexican landscape and Western images while living in Abiquiu.

O'Keeffe's work appears in museums all over the world. A museum in Santa Fe is dedicated just to her art. Not all the state's museums, however, focus on art. The Bradbury Science Museum in Los Alamos explores the state's role in building the first atomic bomb. The museum also has other exhibits related to science. Socorro is the home of a mineral museum, at the New Mexico Institute of Mining and Technology. And the state has several museums of natural history, including one in Las Cruces.

Literature

One of the first writers to settle in New Mexico was Mary Austin. Known for her books on nature and Native

Enduring Adobe

When the Spanish first reached New Mexico, they saw adobe homes everywhere. Adobe is perfect for a hot climate. During summer, the bricks keep out heat from outside. During winter, adobe keeps heat trapped inside the home. The Spanish borrowed the adobe style for their own buildings. Adobe churches from colonial times can still be found across the state, and some modern buildings are made to look like traditional adobe.

Americans, she moved to Santa Fe in 1924 and lived there for ten years. Other well-known writers of that era, such as Willa Cather and D. H. Lawrence, also spent time in New Mexico.

In more recent years, other notable New Mexico writers have emerged. Tony Hillerman is famous for his mystery novels set on the Navajo reservation. The books of M. Scott Momaday reflect the mixture of Native, Anglo, and Hispanic cultures in New Mexico. Rudolfo Anaya's award-winning essays and children's books focus on Hispanic culture.

Music, Theater, and Film

New Mexico has a reputation for welcoming creative people, and the state has a variety of places to enjoy music and theater in both Spanish and English. In Santa Fe, an open-air opera house attracts opera fans from all over the country. Albuquerque has two major concert halls, the Popejoy Hall and the KiMo Theater, where music and theater are staged. One frequent group of performers at the Popejoy is the New Mexico Symphony Orchestra, which formed in 1932.

Motion pictures have a long history in New Mexico. In 1898, Thomas Edison shot the first film made in the state. Since then, dozens of films have been shot there. Many are westerns, but the state has also been the setting for modern

Not Just for the Kitchen

New Mexicans love their chiles, whether they are red or green, hot or mild. Now, there is a new use for hot peppers. Scientists in Chicago and at New Mexico Institute of Mining and Technology have created a substance that repels certain harmful insects and snails using capsaicin, the chemical in chiles that gives them their heat.

▼ The New Mexico Museum of Natural History in Albuquerque traces the development of Earth, starting twelve billion years ago.

comedies and dramas. The 1996 hit film *Independence Day* was partially shot in New Mexico. Based on the novel by New Mexican writer John Nichols, *The Milagro Beanfield War* was shot in northern New Mexico in 1988.

Since the 1980s, a number of Hollywood stars, including Julia Roberts, have bought property in New Mexico. The Taos Talking Picture Festival honors Hollywood stars and features Native American and Hispanic filmmakers.

▲ Artist Georgia O'Keeffe owned homes in Abiquiu and at nearby Ghost Ranch.

Communications

New Mexico has almost two dozen daily newspapers and approximately sixty papers that are published less often, from twice a week to once a month. Some of these papers are written and published by students at the state's colleges and universities. The state's largest paper is the *Albuquerque Journal*. Companies in that city and in Santa Fe also publish a number of monthly magazines. New Mexico has more than one hundred radio stations and nineteen television stations. Most of the TV broadcasts come from Albuquerque.

Sports

New Mexico does not have any major league sports teams, but it does have several minor league teams. The New Mexico Scorpions, based in Albuquerque, play in the Central Hockey League. For years, the minor league baseball team, the Albuquerque Dukes, was part of the Los Angeles Dodgers system, but the team was bought in 2000 and moved to Oregon. In 2001, another minor league team, the Calgary Cannons, moved to the city. Like the Dukes, the new team — renamed the Isotopes — is a Triple-A

DID YOU KNOW?

In 1915, Tom Mix, a top rodeo performer and film actor, came to New Mexico. He shot several Westerns in the state. Mix was famous for doing all of his own stunts on film.

team, just one step below the majors. Albuquerque spent $10 million to improve the city's Sports Stadium for its new team, which was scheduled to begin play in 2003.

Sports fans across the state often root for the Lobos, the athletic teams at the University of New Mexico. Both the men's and women's basketball programs are among the best in the nation. The university's other major sports include baseball, football, soccer, volleyball, golf, and softball.

New Mexico's greatest sports family may be the Unsers. Bobby and Al Unser, brothers born in Albuquerque, were two of the greatest race car drivers of all time. Bobby won his first Indianapolis 500 in 1968; Al's first win at one of the world's greatest tracks came two years later. Between them, the brothers won the race seven times.

New Mexico has become a center for hot-air ballooning, whether for short trips over the state or longer voyages across oceans. In 1978, Maxie Anderson, Ben Abruzzo, and Larry Newman, all from Albuquerque, made the first balloon flight across the Atlantic Ocean. Three years later, Abruzzo and Newman were part of the crew that made the first flight across the Pacific. Anderson also attempted the world's first trip around the world by balloon, but he did not make it. An international balloon museum in Albuquerque is named for Anderson and Abruzzo.

New Mexicans enjoy a wide range of recreational sports. The Taos area has some of the world's best ski slopes. In summer, people enjoy rafting on the Rio Grande and the state's other rivers. New Mexico also offers many opportunities for hunting and fishing.

New Mexico Great

Nancy Lopez was one of the first female Hispanic sports stars in the United States. Born in 1958, she grew up in Roswell and showed tremendous golf skills at an early age. At twelve, she won the New Mexico Women's Amateur Championship. In 1972, she won the first of two U.S. Junior Girls Championships. Roswell's Goddard High School did not have a girls' golf team so Lopez played for the boys, twice leading the team to the state championship. As a professional golfer, she has won more than forty tournaments. Inducted into the LPGA Hall of Fame in 1989, Lopez has been called a great role model for Hispanics and women of all ethnic backgrounds.

▶ Taos is known for great skiing as well as its art. Taos Ski Valley has been called one of the best ski resorts in the world. Every winter, its slopes receive up to 300 inches (762 cm) of light, powdery snow.

Great New Mexicans

> Throughout its long history, New Mexico has meant many things to many people.
>
> — *New Mexican historian, Marc Simmons,*
> New Mexico: An Interpretative History, *1988*

Following are only a few of the thousands of people who were born, died, or spent much of their lives in New Mexico and made extraordinary contributions to the state and the nation.

JUAN DE OÑATE
EXPLORER

BORN: *c. 1550, Zacatecas, Mexico*
DIED: *June 3, 1626, Spain*

Juan de Oñate was the son of a conquistador, one of the Spanish soldiers who seized Mexico for their country. A wealthy and powerful man, Oñate used his own money to fund an expedition to what is now New Mexico in 1598. He led the first European settlers into the Southwest. After starting a small colony at the San Juan Pueblo, Oñate moved on, exploring parts of Texas, the Great Plains, Arizona, and California. During these trips, conditions at San Juan turned bad for the settlers, and most returned to Mexico. When he got back to New Mexico, Oñate made plans for the new town of Santa Fe, but returned to Mexico before it was built. He was charged with several crimes, including using excessive force against New Mexico's Native Americans. Found guilty, Oñate spent most of the rest of his life trying to clear his name.

KIT CARSON
FRONTIERSMAN

BORN: *December 24, 1809, Madison County, KY*
DIED: *May 23, 1868, Fort Lyon, CO*

Christopher "Kit" Carson has been called one of America's great folk heroes. He spent most of his childhood in Missouri, before running away from home when he was fifteen. Carson left for Santa Fe with some traders and spent many years in northern New Mexico. From 1828 to 1831, he used Taos as a base for fur-trapping expeditions. Carson spent much of his time with Native Americans, and he twice married Native American women. During the 1840s, he guided U.S. soldiers through the Rocky Mountains to California, developing a reputation for bravery and honesty. Carson then returned to New Mexico to ranch, although he left several more times to trap and trade goods. On one trip, he was captured by Native Americans and was almost killed. A friendly chief finally ordered his release. During the Civil War, he helped organize New Mexican soldiers loyal to the Union to fight the Confederates. He also fought in the Indian Wars against the Navajo. Today, Carson's former home in Taos is a tourist attraction.

JEAN BAPTISTE LAMY
RELIGIOUS LEADER
BORN: *October 11, 1814, Lempdes, France*
DIED: *February 14, 1888, Santa Fe*

In 1851, Father Jean Baptiste Lamy arrived in New Mexico after doing missionary work in Ohio. Two years later, he started the first school in Santa Fe that taught English. The Roman Catholic Church named him the first bishop of Santa Fe in 1853, and he was later named archbishop. Lamy tried to reform the Spanish-speaking priests of New Mexico, forcing them to follow church rules on proper behavior. Some of these efforts upset the priests and their Hispanic supporters, but Lamy refused to back down. He also built dozens of churches and Catholic schools in the New Mexico territory. In 1927, novelist Willa Cather wrote a novel based on Lamy's life, *Death Comes for the Archbishop.*

BILLY THE KID
OUTLAW
BORN: *November 23, 1859, New York, NY*
DIED: *July 13, 1881, Fort Sumner*

Billy the Kid is part of the myths and legends of the Wild West. He was born in New York, probably named Henry McCarty, although most knew him as Willian H. Bonney. By some accounts, he killed twenty-one men during his short life. Others say he shot many, but only four died. An orphan, Billy came west to work as a ranch hand, ending up in Lincoln County. In 1878, he took part in the Lincoln County War after his boss was killed by rival ranchers. Wanted for several killings, Billy went on the run, but he was caught in 1880 by Sheriff Pat Garrett. Sentenced to die, Billy escaped from jail, but Garrett tracked him down and killed him. Billy the Kid has been the subject of books, films, songs, and even a ballet. Some people think he was a ruthless killer, but others think that his evil reputation is undeserved.

OCTAVIANO LARRAZOLO
POLITICIAN
BORN: *December 7, 1859, Allende, Mexico*
DIED: *April 7, 1930, Albuquerque*

Although he served in the U.S. Senate for less than six months, Octaviano Ambrosio Larrazolo is remembered as the first Hispanic American to serve in that house of Congress. As a boy, he moved to Arizona before going to college in New Mexico. After graduating in 1877, Larrazolo moved to Texas, where he taught and served as a principal before entering politics and becoming a lawyer. Returning to New Mexico in 1895, he began practicing law in Las Vegas. Active in New Mexican politics, he helped make sure the state constitution included legal guarantees for people of Spanish descent. In 1918, running as a Republican, Larrazolo was elected governor of New Mexico. In 1928, while serving in the state house of representatives, Larrazolo was elected to replace Andieus Jones, who had died while serving in the U.S. Senate. Larrazolo soon became ill himself, and he returned to New Mexico shortly before his death.

ELFEGO BACA

GUNFIGHTER AND LAWYER

BORN: *February 10, 1865, Socorro*
DIED: *August 27, 1945, Albuquerque*

As a young man on the New Mexico frontier, Elfego Baca was known for his fast gun and deadly aim. As a sheriff at age nineteen, he single-handedly held off eighty cowboys who had come to free one of their gang whom Baca had just arrested. Baca stayed in a small log hut for more than a day, firing at the outlaws outside. They shot at him through large gaps in the walls but missed. Baca, meanwhile, killed four of the criminals and wounded eight others. In 1894, he became an attorney, specializing in defending poor Hispanics unfairly accused of crimes. Baca also held a number of political offices in New Mexico.

MARIA MARTINEZ

POTTER

BORN: *c. 1887, San Ildefonso Pueblo*
DIED: *July 22, 1980, San Ildefonso Pueblo*

Maria Antonia Montoya Martinez learned the ancient Pueblo art of pottery by watching her aunt. Pottery making was dying out among the women of San Ildefonso, but Maria and her husband Julian Martinez preserved the old methods and sparked new interest in the art. Maria made the pots while Julian painted them. Starting in 1904, the pair traveled across the United States demonstrating their craft. Their most famous pieces featured different shades of black. Maria Martinez often signed her early pieces Marie, after someone suggested that the Anglo form of her name would be more popular. Later, she switched to Maria. In her later years, after Julian died, she often worked with other family members. Martinez's pottery is now prized across the United States.

PETER HURD

ARTIST

BORN: *February 22, 1904, Roswell*
DIED: *July 9, 1984, Roswell*

Peter Hurd went east for his education as an artist, but he returned to his native state to do most of his work. Hurd studied with the well-known illustrator N. C. Wyeth and eventually married Wyeth's daughter Henriette, who was also a painter. The Hurds came to New Mexico during the 1930s, and Peter Hurd often included the state's mountains and deserts in his work. During World War II, Hurd illustrated battle scenes for *Life* magazine. Today, his paintings hang in some of the most famous art museums in the United States.

TONY HILLERMAN
AUTHOR

BORN: *May 27, 1925, Sacred Heart, OK*

As a boy in Oklahoma, Tony Hillerman grew up with many Native American friends. When he became a novelist, he created a Navajo detective, Joe Leaphorn, as the main hero of his mysteries. Hillerman came to New Mexico in 1952 to work as a journalist. For nine years, he was a newspaper editor in Santa Fe. Hillerman then turned to fiction, and he used the Navajo reservation and other parts of the Southwest as the setting for his popular and award-winning books. Hillerman now lives in Albuquerque.

N. SCOTT MOMADAY
AUTHOR

BORN: *February 27, 1934, Lawton, OK*

A member of the Kiowa, Navarre Scott Momaday grew up on Pueblo, Apache, and Navajo reservations in New Mexico and Arizona before his parents settled down at Jemez Pueblo. Momaday had many Hispanic and Anglo friends, and his books reflect the mixture of cultures he has known in his life. His 1968 novel, *House Made of Dawn*, is set at

Jemez Pueblo. The book won a Pulitzer Prize, and Momaday has won other honors for his work. He writes both fiction and poetry and teaches at the University of Arizona. Momaday has also served as a narrator for several projects relating to the West and Native Americans, including the Public Broadcasting System series *The West*.

SID GUTIERREZ
ASTRONAUT

BORN: *June 27, 1951, Albuquerque*

Sidney M. Gutierrez's lifelong dream to fly in space came true in 1991, when he

piloted the space shuttle *Columbia*. Three years later, he was commander of the shuttle *Endeavour*, the first Hispanic American to lead a space shuttle mission. After graduating from Albuquerque's Valley High School, Gutierrez attended the U.S. Air Force Academy and then became an Air Force pilot, flying about thirty different types of aircraft. The National Aeronautics and Space Administration (NASA) selected Gutierrez as an astronaut in 1984. When he retired from NASA in 1994, he returned to Albuquerque to work at Sandia National Laboratories.

New Mexico
History At-A-Glance

1539
Marcos de Niza leads an expedition to the Zuni village of Hawikúh.

1598
Juan de Oñate starts the first Spanish colony in what is now New Mexico.

1610
The Palace of the Governors is built in Santa Fe.

1680
Popé leads a Pueblo uprising against the Spanish.

1692
The Spanish regain control of northern New Mexico.

1706
Albuquerque is founded.

1821
New Mexico becomes part of the newly independent country of Mexico.

1822
Opening of the Santa Fe Trail.

1848
The United States acquires New Mexico after winning the Mexican War.

1862
Union forces drive Confederate troops out of New Mexico.

1878–81
Rival ranchers and merchants fight the Lincoln County War.

1881
Billy the Kid killed, at Fort Sumner.

1600   **1700**   **1800**

1492
Christopher Columbus comes to New World.

1607
Capt. John Smith and three ships land on Virginia coast and start first English settlement in New World — Jamestown.

1754–63
French and Indian War.

1773
Boston Tea Party.

1776
Declaration of Independence adopted July 4.

1777
Articles of Confederation adopted by Continental Congress.

1787
U.S. Constitution written.

1812–14
War of 1812.

United States
History At-A-Glance

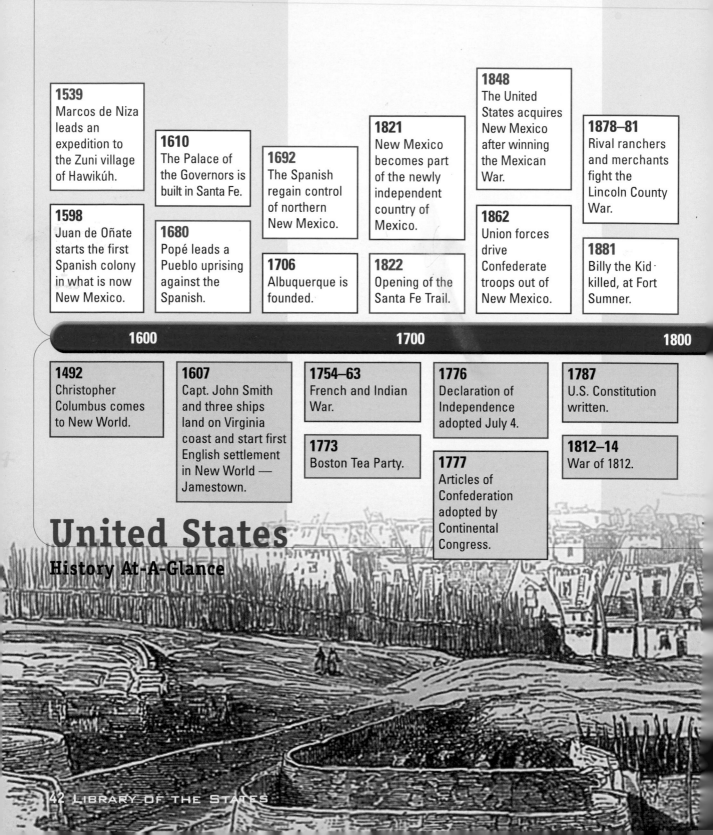

1911
New Mexico adopts a state constitution.

1912
New Mexico enters the Union as the forty-seventh state.

1928
Octaviano Larrazolo becomes the first Hispanic American to serve in the U.S. Senate.

1930
Robert Goddard begins testing rockets in the desert near Roswell.

1930s
The U.S. government builds dams that provide jobs and water for farms.

1943
The U.S. government sends scientists to Los Alamos to begin building an atomic bomb.

1945
The world's first atomic bomb explodes at the Trinity Site near Alamogordo.

1948
Native Americans win the right to vote in state elections.

1950
Uranium is discovered near Grants.

1970
Al Unser wins the first of four Indianapolis 500 auto races.

1997
Georgia O'Keeffe Museum opens in Santa Fe.

2000
Computer chip maker Intel begins a $2 billion expansion in Rio Rancho.

1800 · · · **1900** · · · **2000**

1848
Gold discovered in California draws eighty thousand prospectors in the 1849 Gold Rush.

1861–65
Civil War.

1869
Transcontinental railroad completed.

1917–18
U.S. involvement in World War I.

1929
Stock market crash ushers in Great Depression.

1941–45
U.S. involvement in World War II.

1950–53
U.S. fights in the Korean War.

1964–73
U.S. involvement in Vietnam War.

2000
George W. Bush wins the closest presidential election in history.

2001
A terrorist attack in which four hijacked airliners crash into New York City's World Trade Center, the Pentagon, and farmland in western Pennsylvania leaves thousands dead or injured.

▼ This woodcut print shows the streets of Santa Fe in 1860.

Festivals and Fun for All

Check web site for exact date and directions.

Albuquerque International Balloon Fiesta, Albuquerque

Every October, the skies over Albuquerque fill with more than one thousand colorful hot-air balloons during the largest festival of its kind in the world. The city's unique weather conditions and location in the mountains make it an ideal spot for flying balloons. The fiesta's events include balloon races and fireworks.
www.aibf.org

Chile Festival, Hatch

Hatch calls itself the chile capital of the world, and each year it hosts a festival featuring lots of spicy food, a parade, carnival rides, music, and the crowning of the festival queen.
www.southernnewmexico.com/ snm/chilfest.html

Christmas on the Pecos, Carlsbad

Carlsbad may not have much snow in December, but it does have a bright celebration of the holiday season. Homeowners along the Pecos River string up thousands of colorful lights, which residents and guests view from boats that slowly sail along the waterway.
www.chamber.caverns.com/xmas.htm

Feast Day, San Ildefonso

The Tewa of San Ildefonso, like the other Pueblo Indians of New Mexico, hold an annual public feast. This one falls on January 23, and the ceremonies begin the night before with a large bonfire. During the feast, dancers honor the buffalo, which the Native Americans once hunted for food. Corn, another important part of the Pueblo diet, also plays an important role in the ceremonies. Visitors are not allowed to take pictures of Native dancers at any of the pueblos in New Mexico.
www.sidecanyon.com/ features/events3.htm

Festival of the Cranes, Socorro

Each year, thousands of cranes — including rare whooping cranes — come to Bosque del Apache National Wildlife Refuge to spend the winter. The festival welcomes the birds to their winter home while educating the public about the wildlife refuge.
www.friendsofthebosque.org

Fiesta de Santa Fe, Santa Fe

This citywide celebration is the oldest of its kind in the United States. The first fiesta was held in 1712 to mark the twentieth

anniversary of the return of Spanish control to New Mexico. Today, the fiesta pays tribute to both history and fun. A highlight is the burning of Zozobra, or "Old Man Gloom," a 40-foot (12-m) figure made out of wood and cloth.
www.santafefiesta.org

Great American Duck Race, Deming

This wacky, quacky event was first held in 1980. Ducks race on land and in water, with the winners earning cash prizes. Their human handlers get in on the fun too. They can dress up as ducks for the Duck Royalty Pageant or take part in the tortilla toss or outhouse race.
www.demingduckrace.com

Indian Market, Santa Fe

Tens of thousands of people come each year for the Indian Market. The world's largest sale of Native American art features craftspeople from more than one hundred tribes. The weekend also includes an auction and a Native American clothing contest.
www.swaia.org/indianmrkt.html

Inter-Tribal Indian Ceremonial, Gallup

One of the largest gatherings of North American tribes, the ceremonial features Indian crafts, food, dancing, rodeos, and educational activities for non-Indian visitors.
www.gallupnm.org/ ceremonial/info.htm

New Mexico State Fair, Albuquerque

Called one of the ten best state fairs in the country, the New Mexico State Fair — which takes place in mid-September — has a wide assortment of rides, food, and entertainment. One of the highlights is a rodeo, and the fair also has horse races.
www.nmstatefair.com

• •
▶ Many festivals and celebrations in New Mexico include Native Americans dressed in traditional costumes.

Old Taos Trade Festival, Taos

This annual event re-creates a slice of Taos life from the nineteenth century, when trappers and traders met in the town. The festival has music, food, crafts, and people dressed in costume.
www.taoschamber.com

Taos Spring Arts Festival, Taos

This festival is one of two held every year in Taos that features the work of local artists. The festival also attracts dancers and theater groups from other parts of the country and local entertainers who highlight the cultural diversity of northern New Mexico.
www.taoschamber.com

UFO Festival, Roswell

Each July 4th weekend, Roswell hosts a UFO event that explores everything alien with lectures, music, and games. Visitors can bring homemade models of spaceships and discuss the famous "Roswell incident" of 1947.
www.uforoswell.com

Winter Spanish Market, Santa Fe

A tribute to New Mexico's Spanish roots, this celebration offers modern examples of traditional Hispanic folk art. Some 120 New Mexican artists take part. Visitors can visit the studios of artists based in Santa Fe. The market also has food and dancing.
www.spanishmarket.org

New Mexico 47

Books

Griego y Maestas, José and Anaya, Rudolfo A. *Cuentos: Tales from the Hispanic Southwest*. Santa Fe: Museum of New Mexico Press, 1980. A collection of Hispanic folktales from New Mexico and southern Colorado, presented in both English and Spanish.

Keegan, Marcia. *Pueblo Girls: Growing Up in Two Worlds*. Santa Fe: Clear Light Publications, 1999. Two sisters from the San Ildefonso Pueblo tell how they combine their family's traditional ways with modern American culture.

Litchman, Kristin Embry. *Secrets of a Los Alamos Kid: 1946–1953*. Los Alamos: Los Alamos Historical Society, 2001. The daughter of a scientist who worked at the Los Alamos National Laboratory recalls her childhood during the Cold War, when the United States was trying to build bigger and better atomic weapons.

Simmons, Marc. *New Mexico!* Albuquerque: University of New Mexico Press, 1997. A well-known historian of New Mexico offers young readers a detailed look at the people and places of the state, from the ancient past to today.

Vivian, R. Gwinn, and Margaret J. Anderson. *Chaco Canyon*. New York: Oxford University Press, 2002. A look at the ruins at Chaco Canyon and the people who once lived there.

Web Sites

▶ Official state web site
www.state.nm.us

▶ City of Santa Fe web site
http://sfweb.ci.santa-fe.nm.us

▶ Southern New Mexico Online
www.southernnewmexico.com

▶ Navajo Nation homepage
www.navajo.org

▶ Carlsbad Caverns National Park
www.nps.gov/cave

Films and Documentaries

Colonial Life: The Spanish and Colonial Santa Fe. Schlessinger Media, 1999. A documentary on Spanish rule in Santa Fe.

Milagro Beanfield War. MCA Home Video, 1988. Directed by Robert Redford, this fictional film looks at farm life in northern New Mexico.

Note: Page numbers in *italics* refer to maps, illustrations, or photographs.

A

Abruzzo, Ben, 37
Acoma Pueblo, 7, 10
adobe, 8, 34
African Americans, *17*
age distribution, 16
agriculture, 8, 9, 24, *25*, 26, 27
airport, 27
Alamorgordo, NM, 15
Albuquerque International Balloon Fiesta, 44, *44*
Albuquerque International Sunport, 27
Albuquerque Journal, 36
Albuquerque, NM, 6, 11, 14, 18, 26, 27, 33, 35, 37, 42, 45
Allen, Paul, 26
Altair 8800, 26
Anasazi Indians, 4, 8, *9*, *13*, 13, 21, 32–33
Anaya, Rudolf, 35
Anderson, Maxie, 37
Anglos, 4, 12–13, 16–17, *17*, 18–19, 32
animals, *20*, *21*, 23
Apache Indians, 9, 17
art, 4, 15, 32–34, 45. *See also* O'Keefe, Georgia
atomic bomb, 7, 14, *14*, 15, 43
attorney general, 29
attractions, 7, *44*, 44–45, *45*. *See also* culture; parks
Austin, Mary, 34–35

B

Baca, Elfego, 40
ballad (state), 6
balloons. *See* hot-air ballooning
Bandelier National Monument, *12*, 12, 21
Becknell, William, *11*, 11
Bent, Charles, 12
Billy the Kid, 39, *39*, 42
Bingaman, Jeff, 31
bird (state), 6, *6*
black bear, 6
blue grama (state grass), 6, 20
Bonney, William H., *39*, 39
Bosque del Apache National Wildlife Refuge, 44
Bradbury Science Museum, 34

C

Calgary Cannons, 36
Canadian River, 20, 23

capital. *See* Santa Fe, NM
capitol building, *29*, 29
capsaicin, 35
Capulin Volcano National Monument, 21
Carlsbad Caverns National Park, 7, *21*, 21
Carlsbad, NM, 44
Carson, Christopher "Kit", *38*, 38–39
casinos, 27
Cather, Willa, 35, 39
Catholic schools, 19
cattle, 13–14, 24
Chaco Culture National Historic Park, *9*, 9
chaparral, 23
Chicanos, 17
Chihuahuan Desert, 21
chile (pepper), 6, 26, 35
Chile Festival, 44
Christianity, 11, 19, 39
Christmas on the Pecos, 44
Cibola, 9, 10
Cimarron, NM, 13
Civil War, 13
Cody, Buffalo Bill, 13
coelophysis (state fossil), 6
College of Santa Fe, 19
Columbia space shuttle, 41
commissioner of public lands, 29
communications, 36
Conchas Lake, 21
Constitution, New Mexico State, 28, 43
Cook, Don, 6
Coronado, Francisco Vásquez de, 10
counties, 31
culture, *32*, 32–37, *33*, *34*, *36*, *37*

D

Death Comes for the Archbishop (Cather), 39
Deming, NM, 45
Domenici, Pete, 31

E

economy, 24–27, *25*, *26*, *27*
Edison, Thomas, 35
education, 18, 19
El Camino Real, 7
El Rancho de las Golondrinas, 7
Elephant Butte Lake, 21
Endeavour shuttle, 41
Endlich, Frederic M., 24
Estevanico, 9

events, *44*, 44–45, *45*
executive branch, 28–30

F

farming. *See* agriculture
Feast Day, 44
Festival of the Cranes, 44
festivals, *44*, 44–45, *45*
Fiesta de Santa Fe, *32*, 44–45
films, 35–36
fish, 6, 23
flag (state), *6*
flower (state), *6*, 6
foreign-born groups, *16*
forestry, *25*, 26
forests, 21, 22
fossil (state), 6
Four Corners, 22
frijoles (beans), 6

G

Gallup, NM, 45
Garrett, Elizabeth, 6
Garrett, Pat, 39
Gates, Bill, 26
gem (state), 6
geography. *See* land
Georgia O'Keefe Museum, 43
Gila National Forest, 21
Gila River, 21
Goddard, Robert, 15, *15*, 43
Gorman, R.C., 33
government, 28–31, *29*, *31*. *See also* U.S. government
governor, 28–29
grass (state), 6, 20
Great American Duck Race, 45
Great Depression, 14
Great Plains, 20–21
gross state product, *25*
Gutierrez, Sid, 41, *41*
gypsum, 7

H

Hatch, NM, 44
Hawikúh, 9
"The Heart of New Mexico" (Endlich), 24
heritage, 4, *16*, 16–17, 32
High Plateau, 21–22
Hillerman, Tony, 35, 41
Hispanics, 4, 14, 16–17, *17*, 18, 19, 32, 33–34, 37, 39–40, 41, *41*
history, 8–15, *9*, *10*, *11*, *12*, *13*, *14*, *15*, 42–43
hot-air ballooning, 37, 44, *44*
Hot Foot Teddy, 7
House Made of Dawn (Momaday), 41

house of representatives, 30
Hurd, Peter, *40*, 40–41

I

immigration, 16
Independence Day (movie), 35–36
Indian Market, 45
Indian Pueblo Cultural Center, 33
insect (state), 6
Intel, 26, 43
interstate highways, 27
Inter-tribal Indian Ceremonial, 45
Isotopes, 36

J

James, Thomas, 16
Jemez mountain range, 21
Jemez Pueblo, 41
Jewish population, 19
Jones, Andieus, 40
judicial branch, 30–31

K

Kearny, Stephen, 8, 12, 28
KiMo Theater, 35
kivas, 19
Kokopelli, 33

L

lakes, 21
Lamy, Jean Baptiste, 39
Lamy, NM, 39
land, 4, 6, *20–21*, 20–23, *22*, *23*
"Land of Enchantment", 4
"Land of Enchantment, The" (state ballad), 6
Larrazolo, Octaviano Ambrosio, 39–40, 43
Las Cruces, NM, 6
Lawrence, D.H., *20*, 35
Leaphorn, Joe, 41
legislative branch, 30
lieutenant governor, 29
Lincoln County War, 14, 39, 42
Lincoln National Forest, 7
Lindbergh, Charles, 15
literature, 34–35, 41
livestock, 24, *26*, 26
López, George, 33–34
Lopez, Nancy, 37, *37*
Los Alamos, 34, 43
Lucero, Amadeo, 6
lumber, 26

M

mammal (state), 6
manufacturing, *25*, 26–27

maps, *5, 22, 25*
Martinez, Julian, 40
Martinez, Maria Antonia
     Montoya, 40, *40*
McCarty, Henry, 39, *39*
Mexican-American War, 4
Mexican Revolution, 12
Mexican War, 12–13
Mexico, 11, 42
Milagro Beanfield War, The
     (movie), 36
Mimbres Indians, 8, 32
mining, 13, 24, *25*, 26, *27*, 27
missionaries, 11, 39
Mix, Tom, 36
Mogollon Indians, 8
Momaday, M. Scott, 35, 41,
     41
Montoya, Joseph, *31*, 31
motto (state), 6
The Mountain on the Desert
     (Richter), 32
Murphy, Michael Martin, 6
Museum of Indian Arts and
     Culture, 33
Museum of Natural History,
     35, *35*
Museum of Spanish Colonial
     Art, 34
museums, 33–34, *35*, 35
music, *34*, 35

N
NASA (National Aeronautics
     and Space
     Administration), 41
national representation, 31
Native Americans, 4, 8–13, *12,
     13*, 14, 16–17, *17*, 19, *19*,
     19, 24, 26, 27, 31, 32–33.
     See also notable people;
     specific tribe names
natural resources, 26
Navajo (Dineh) Indians, 8–9,
     17, 26–27, 33
Navajo Lake, 21
Newman, Larry, 37
New Mexico: An
     Interpretative History
     (Simmons), 38
New Mexico cutthroat trout, 6
New Mexico Institute of
     Mining and Technology,
     34
New Mexico State
     Constitution, 28, 43
New Mexico State Fair, 45
New Mexico State University,
     19
New Mexico Symphony
     Orchestra, 35
newspapers, 36

Nichols, John, 36
Niza, Marcos de, 9–10, 42
Nuevomexicanos, 17

O
Oakley, Annie, 13
O'Keefe, Georgia, 34, 36, 43
Old Taos Trade Festival, 45
Oñate, Don Juan de, 10, 38, 42

P
Palace of the Governors,
     Santa Fe, 7, *31*, 31, 42
parks, 7, *9*, 9, 21, *21*, 32, 44
Pecos River, 20, 23
people, notable, 38–41
Perea, José Leandro, 28
Petroglyph National
     Monument, 21, 32
petroglyphs, 13, *13*
Phoenix: The Posthumous
     Papers (Lawrence), 20
piñon (state tree), 6, 22
plants, 20, *21*, 22–23
politics, 31. *See also*
     government
Popé, 11, 42
Popejoy Hall, 35
population, 6, *16*, 16–19, *17*
potash, 26, 27
priests, 11
public regulation
     commissioner, 29–30
pueblo, defined, 11
Pueblo Indians, 9, 11, 13, 16,
     17, 19, 32, 33, *40*, 40, 44

R
religion, 11, 19, 39
research and development
     (R&D), 27
reservations, 9, 13, 17
Richardson, Bill, 31
Richter, Conrad, 32
Rio Grande, 4, *20*, 21, 23, 37
Rio Rancho, NM, 6, 26, 43
rivers, 20, 21, 23
roadrunner, 6, *6*
roads, 7, 27
Roberts, Julia, 36
Rocky Mountains, 21
Roman Catholic Church, 39
Roosevelt, Franklin, 14
Roosevelt, Theodore, 14
Roswell, NM, 6, 7, 15, 26, 27,
     37, 45
"Rough Riders", 14
"Roundhouse", *29*, 29

S
San Gabriel, NM, 10
San Ildefonso Pueblo, 40, 44

San Juan mountain range, 21
San Juan Pueblo, 10, 38
San Juan River, 21
Sandia Indians, 8
Sandia Mountains, 8
Sangre de Cristo mountain
     range, 21
Santa Fe, NM, 4, 6, 11, 30, *32,
     33*, 33, 34, 38, 39, 44–45.
     See also Palace of the
     Governors, Santa Fe
Santa Fe Opera House, *34*, 35
Santa Fe Trail, *10*, 11, 42
Santos, 33
secretary of state, 29
services, 24, *25*, 27
sheep, 24, *26*
Shiprock, 22, *23*
Simmons, Marc, 38
skiing, 37, *37*
"Sky City", 7, 10
Smokey Bear, 7
Socorro, NM, 44
songs (state), 6
Sonoran Desert, 21
Spanish, 9–10, 11, 32, 33–34,
     42, 44–45
Spanish American War, 14
sports, 36–37, *37*
state auditor, 29
state treasurer, 29
statehood, 6, 28

T
Taos, NM, 4, 12, *20*, 37, 39, 45
Taos Ski Valley, 37, *37*
Taos Spring Arts Festival, 45
Taos Talking Picture Festival,
     36
tarantula hawk wasp, 6
technology goods, 26
Tewa Indians, 10
theater, 35
tourism, 27
transportation, *25*, 27
tree (state), 6
Trinity Site, 7, *14*, 14, 43
turquoise, 6, 24

U
UFO Festival, 45
unidentified flying object
     (UFO), 7
Union, 6, 14, 28, 42
United States, 12–13, 42–43
U.S. government, 14–15, 19,
     24, *25*, 43
U.S. House of
     Representatives, 31
U.S. military, 7
University of New Mexico, 19
Unser, Al, 37, 43

Unser, Bobby, 37
uranium, 26, 43
Ute Mountain tribe, 9

V
Valverde, 13
vegetables (state), 6, *6*
Vietnam War, 15

W
War of 1812, 11
Web sites, 46
Wheeler Peak, 20, 21
White Sands Missile Range,
     15
White Sands National
     Monument, 7
Wild West, 13–14, 39
Winter Spanish Market, 45
World War I, 14
World War II, 4, 14–15, 41
Wyeth, Henriette, 41
Wyeth, N. C., 41

Y
yucca (state flower), *6*, 6, 23

Z
Zozobra, 44–45
Zuni, 9